Studying Egyptian life

All human beings need food and shelter to survive. They also need things to look forward to that give their lives hope and meaning. Throughout history, different groups of people around the world have come up with their own ways of meeting these basic requirements. Studying past **civilizations** can tell us how people used the resources around them to build shelters, how they found or farmed food, and how they met their spiritual needs and hopes for a better future.

△ Some simple farming methods used by the ancient Egyptians are still used today.

▽ This map shows modern-day Egypt and nearby countries, some of which were of major importance to ancient Egypt.

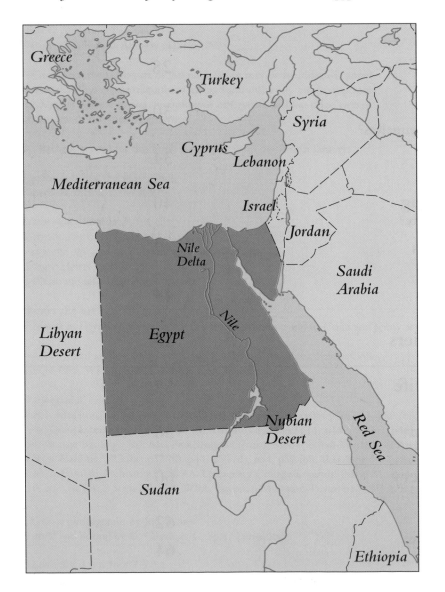

IN THE COURSE OF HISTORY civilizations have risen and eventually fallen because of internal troubles or pressures from outside. The story of the ancient Egyptian civilization is a very long one. It lasted for over 3,000 years. The great Roman Empire rose and fell in half that time, and the Greek civilization lasted less than 1,000 years.

TO HELP people make sense of this vast stretch of time, the greatest period of Egyptian history is usually divided into three periods, or kingdoms. In this book we have given each kingdom a symbol, which is used purely as a guide, when information relates to that time.

KEY FOR SYMBOLS

Old Kingdom 2686 BC – 2181 BC

Middle Kingdom 2055 BC – 1650 BC

New Kingdom 1550 BC – 1069 BC

EGYPT'S GEOGRAPHICAL LOCATION plays a vital part in understanding its development as a civilization. During the period covered in this book, foreign trade and travel grew with the discovery of valuable raw materials from abroad.

THE EGYPTIANS travelled to nearby countries by sea or overland. As the wealthiest country of the ancient world, Egypt had much to offer its neighbours, such as gold from the Eastern Desert, in exchange for what it lacked. This made for good trading relations at first, but later led to invasion by foreign countries keen to exploit Egypt's fine natural resources.

EGYPT'S LEGACY to the world lies in some of the most spectacular monuments ever built. The **pyramids** at Giza, the Great Sphinx, and magnificent temples, are all wonderful technological achievements. In fact, many experts are still trying to understand how the Egyptians were able to build such massive constructions with the use of only very simple tools.

ARCHAEOLOGISTS AND ANTHROPOLOGISTS have, however, been able to explain a lot about the daily lifestyle of the ancient Egyptians by the wall-paintings, documents, treasures, personal possessions and household items that have been discovered in the remains of such tombs and temples.

△ *The magnificent temple at Abu Simbel was carved out of sandstone cliffs, for Queen Nefertari, on the orders of Ramses II.*

THESE FINDINGS also reveal much about the Egyptians' religious faith and their views on death and what followed. Experts have been able to work out a lot about their belief in the **afterlife** from the discovery of tomb models buried with the dead, coffins covered with written spells to protect against danger and **mummies** – perfectly preserved bodies for burial.

◁ *This wall-painting shows the type of boats the ancient Egyptians used, the birds found on the banks of the Nile and the tools that noblemen used for hunting.*

THE MAKE IT WORK! way of looking at history is to ask questions of the past and to find the answers by making the things people made, as close as possible to the way they made them. You do not need to make everything in the book to understand the ancient Egyptian's way of life. Simply by looking at the step-by-step instructions, you will be able to see how they put things together and made them work efficiently.

The fertile River Nile

The first Egyptians were **Stone Age** hunters, followed by settlers from the south and east who were attracted by the river valley's fertile soil. The ancient Egyptian civilization began over 5,000 years ago and lasted for 3,000 years, before being wiped out by foreign invasions. Initially Egypt was divided into Upper and Lower Egypt (the valley and the **delta**). These were united in 3118 BC and ruled by a pharaoh called 'Lord of the Two Lands'.

▽ *The compass shows the direction of the flow of the Nile: south to north.*

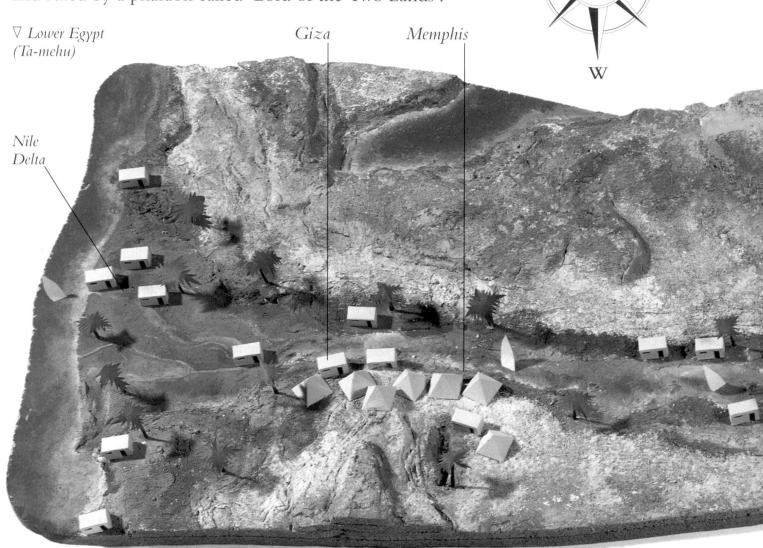

▽ *Lower Egypt (Ta-mehu)*

Giza

Memphis

Nile Delta

THE MARSHY, TRIANGULAR DELTA of Lower Egypt, where the river divides into separate branches, was known as *Ta-mehu* – land of the papyrus plant. Upper Egypt, the long, narrow valley just 11 kilometres wide, was called *Ta-shema* – land of the reed. Ancient Egyptian civilization developed in these two fertile areas.

MEMPHIS was one of the most inhabited areas, not only of Egypt, but of the ancient world. It was the capital of Egypt during the Old Kingdom and its harbour and workshops played a key part in the country's foreign trade. Just north of Memphis is Giza, the site of the largest pyramid of all – the Great Pyramid.

PRIEST:
temples
priest ra
dancers
directly

SCRIBE:
They ac
oversaw
to send
41) so tl
could tl
where t

papyrus

THE SOURCE OF THE NILE is in the lakes and mountain springs of Ethiopia and Central Africa. From there it flows north to the Mediterranean Sea. Summer rains caused the floor of the Nile Valley to flood, creating a lush green corridor. In modern Egypt, the Aswan Dam, built in the 1960s, keeps the level of the Nile constant.

▷ This aerial view shows the Nile Valley today. It is no longer a green strip as in ancient Egypt, because the Aswan Dam holds back the annual flood waters.

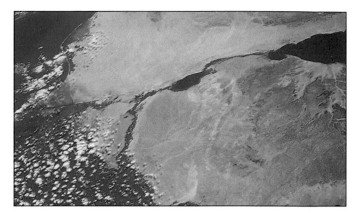

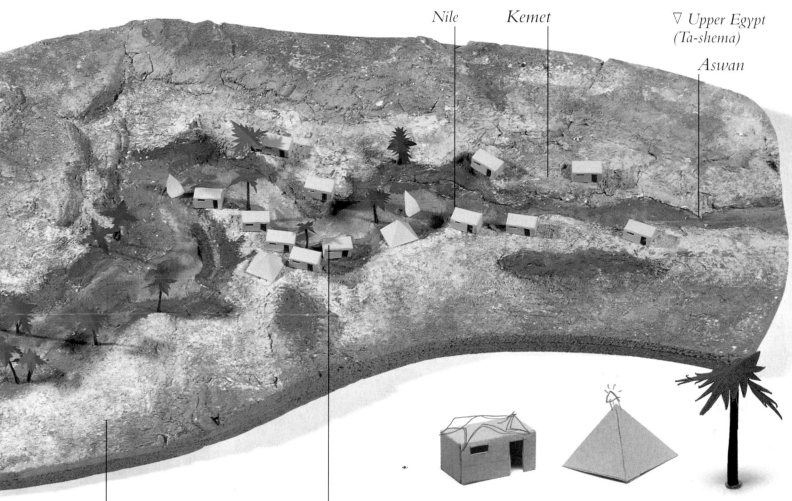

Nile   Kemet   *▽ Upper Egypt (Ta-shema)*

Aswan

Deshret   *Thebes*   *towns*   *monument sites*   *fertile areas*

THE RED LAND or *Deshret* was the desert that surrounded the river valley. There was nothing to sustain life and nobody lived there. For the ancient Egyptians however, it provided several things: a barrier against invasion, safe trade routes to the rest of Africa, sandstone for building monuments and gold for making jewellery.

THE BLACK LAND, known as *Kemet*, was the narrow strip of **silt** that runs along the river valley. It took its name from the rich, fertile soil in which crops flourished. The Egyptians called themselves *remet-en-Kemet* – people of the black land – and their language, *medet-remet-en-Kemet*, meant speech of the people of the black land.

Egypt
admin
judges
or ser
goveri
were t
could

Everyday life

Ancient Egyptians had a strong sense of family, and usually married someone from their own social group or extended family. Historians once thought that brothers and sisters sometimes married, but apart from the royal family, it seems that this was not true. The words 'brother' and 'sister' in ancient Egyptian were simply terms of affection. Marriage was fairly straight-forward and divorce was legal, but costly.

△ *This Old Kingdom tomb model of a woman and her husband, Hetepheres and Kaitep, dates from 2500 BC.*

INTER-MARRIAGES often took place within the extended family, such as between cousins. Children played an important role in society and were thought to be a great blessing. Parents prayed to the gods for many children who were then expected to look after their parents during old age.

CHILDHOOD was short as children were sent to learn a trade, or the privileged few to be educated at scribal school, when they were only eight or nine years old. Girls married when they were as young as 12 years old and boys at 14. The average life expectancy was 40 years, although mummies of officials and rulers show that some lived much longer.

DAILY LIFE centred around the market place, with stalls filling squares and lining streets. This is where the wealthy would send their servants to shop. The ancient Egyptians did not use money, relying instead on a **barter** and exchange system of trade. They used everything for this – from storage jars and furniture to grain, flax or copper ore. Prices rarely went up, which meant that the value of things tended to remain the same. As a result, people knew what to expect in exchange for their goods.

cattle

market stall

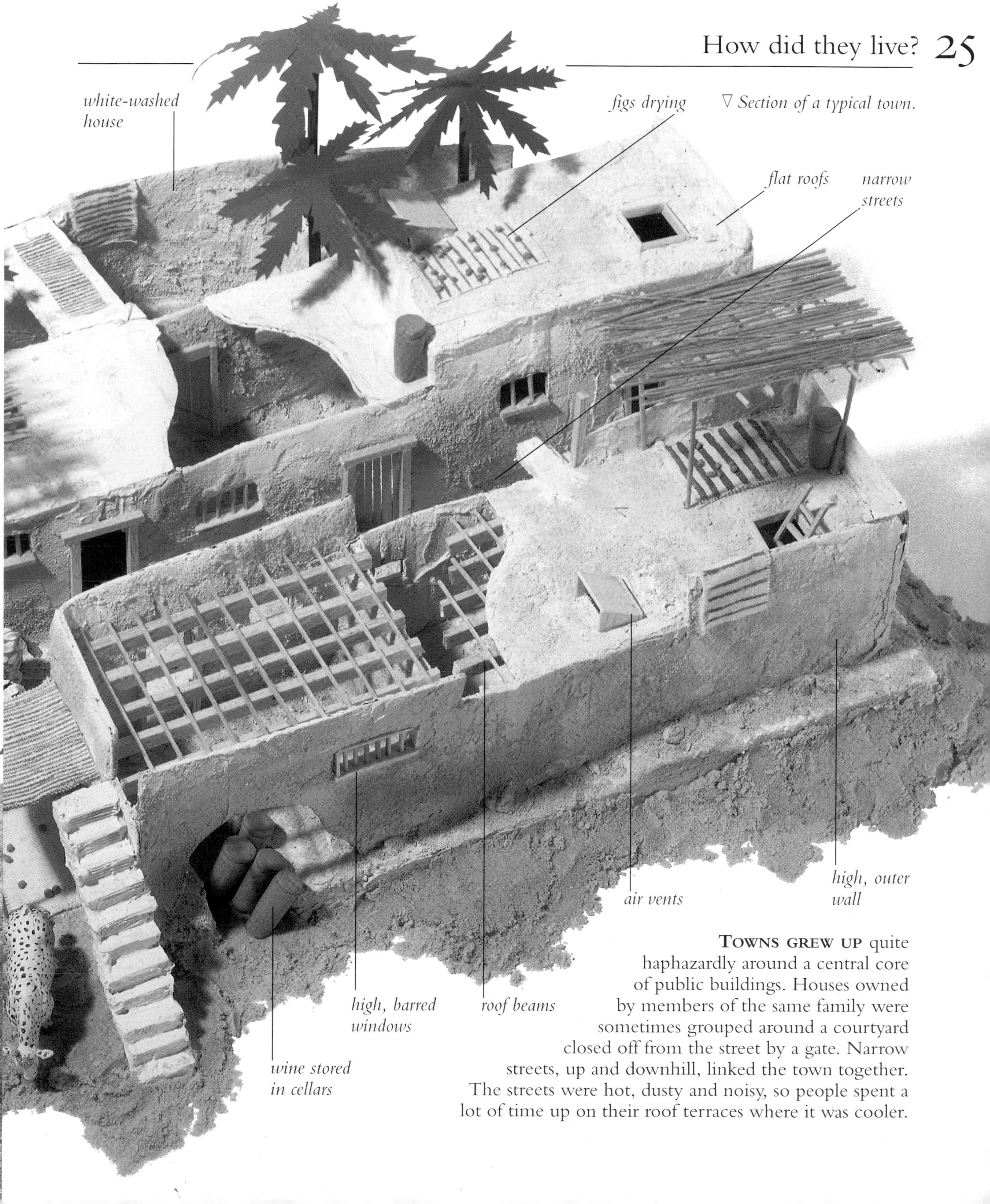

white-washed
house

figs drying

▽ Section of a typical town.

flat roofs

narrow
streets

air vents

high, outer
wall

high, barred
windows

roof beams

wine stored
in cellars

TOWNS GREW UP quite
haphazardly around a central core
of public buildings. Houses owned
by members of the same family were
sometimes grouped around a courtyard
closed off from the street by a gate. Narrow
streets, up and downhill, linked the town together.
The streets were hot, dusty and noisy, so people spent a
lot of time up on their roof terraces where it was cooler.

HUNTING was a favourite pastime of men. The pharaoh and his nobles hunted lions, wild bulls and leopards. Accompanied by professional hunters, they took off into the desert in horse-drawn chariots in pursuit of prey. Alternatively, they would lie in wait around a water hole, ready to attack with bows and arrows.

IN THE MARSHY RIVER DELTA, water birds were killed with throwing sticks, and hippopotami with lassoes and harpoons. Hippos were a menace to farmers as they flattened crops. Only the brave hunted crocodiles!

▷ *Hippo-hunting on the river.*

THE RIVER was also a place to relax. Egyptians would take their reed boats down to the water, enjoy a picnic, go fishing or catch water birds.

CHILDREN played leap-frog and tug-of-war, and practised wrestling and gymnastics. **Senet** was a favourite board game played by everyone.

MAKE A SENET GAME

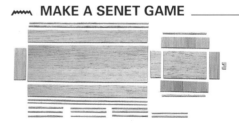

You will need: balsa wood, craft knife, PVA glue, paint, felt-tip pens, self-hardening clay, ruler, sandpaper

1 Ask an adult to help you cut the balsa wood as shown. The larger pieces on the left are for the board, the smaller (right) are for the drawer.

2 Make five pieces each for both players (and a couple of spares), from the clay. When the clay is dry, paint five of the pieces black and the other five white.

3 Glue together the drawer and handle from balsa wood as shown. Then glue the drawer runners to the bottom edge of the side pieces. Mark the top board into 30 squares.

TO PLAY SENET

The object of the game is for one player to get his or her pieces around and off the board before their opponent. Players throw the four dice sticks to find out how far to move when it is their turn:

One flat side up = 1   Four flat sides up = 4
Two flat sides up = 2   Four round sides up = 6
Three flat sides up = 3

RULES

- Throwing a 1, 4 or 6 wins a player another throw.
- Pieces move up and down the board lengthways: row one, left to right; row two, right to left; row three, left to right.
- Landing on a square occupied by an opponent means the opponent's piece must move back to the square his attacker has come from.
- Two pieces of the same colour cannot occupy one square, but next to each other they cannot be attacked.
- Three pieces in a row cannot be passed by an opponent.
- The square marked means a player must go back to the square marked ⚷, and if that is occupied, go back to the start.
- The squares marked ⌇⌇⌇, ⟋⟋⟋ and 👥 are safe from attack.
- A player cannot move a piece off the board until all his pieces are off the first row.

START OF PLAY

1 Place a white piece on every other square of the first row and five black pieces on the squares in between.

2 The first player to throw a 1 moves the last black piece on the first row one square down. Then he throws again, free now to move any of the black pieces.

start

finish

3 When the white player makes his first move, he must use the last white piece in the first row.

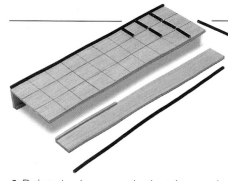

4 Paint the long vertical strips and shorter dividing sticks black. Cut the dividing sticks into short strips and glue firmly in between the vertical ones as shown above.

5 Copy the images above on to the top of the board. It is important that each sits on the correct square as shown right. Decorate the board's sides with felt-tip pens and paint.

6 Cut four more short, thin strips from the balsa wood to use as throwing sticks. Sand one side of each stick to a rounded shape and then paint the other side brown.

Pyramids and burial

Pharaohs believed that they became gods in the afterlife, so their tombs had to be very grand. Pyramid tombs were built during the Old Kingdom. The shape represents the mound of earth that rose out of the dark ocean at the beginning of time, from which the creator god Re emerged (see page 52). The biggest pyramid is the Great Pyramid of Giza. It is still one of the largest man-made structures in the world.

△ The Great Pyramid of Giza was the burial tomb of the pharaoh Cheops. It took over 20 years to build, and originally stood at 146m.

△ Some experts believe that a long, shallow, mud and rubble ramp was used to haul huge building blocks up to the pyramid on sledges.

△ As the pyramid got higher, the ramp would get longer, to keep an even gradient.

covered causeway, nearly 1km long

valley temple

Nile

MARKING OUT the ground was the first step. It involved complex mathematics. To set out the corner blocks, the height of the pyramid and the angle of the sloping sides had to be calculated carefully. This ensured that the top would be dead centre.

TO CUT STONES the Egyptians used copper and bronze tools (iron was very scarce). Another method was to make small holes in a block of stone, along the line to be cut. Wooden wedges were forced into the holes and water was poured over the dry wood to make it swell up and crack the stone along the line.

TO SMOOTH THE SURFACE of the pyramid, great triangular facing blocks of the best quality polished limestone were cut and added to each course, from the top down. These facing stones gleamed white in the sun. The stone cutters were so skilful at cutting and fitting the blocks (they did not use cement) that even today a piece of paper cannot be slipped between two blocks.

◁ *Pyramid complex of Sahure at Abusir.*

pyramid for the queen

enclosure wall

mortuary temple

ARCHAEOLOGISTS have various theories on how the Egyptians heaved two-and-a-half-tonne stone blocks up a pyramid.

THE FIRST LAYER, or course, of stones was laid out all over the base. Side blocks were then laid out, meeting each of the corner stones. The next course was laid on the first, and so on up to 200 courses, until a single capping stone was placed on top. (In the case of the Great Pyramid of Giza, this was coated in gold.) Meanwhile, tomb chambers, ante-rooms and access tunnels inside the pyramid were beaten out of the blocks with hammers made of a hard stone called dolerite.

THE ONE RAMP THEORY suggests that a mud ramp was built and the stones dragged up it. But for the angle of the ramp to be shallow enough, it would have had to be three times as long as the pyramid, and no rubble has been found to indicate that such a structure ever existed.

THE ANGLED RAMP THEORY states that the internal core of the pyramid was built in steps and series of ramps were built, from step to step. The steps were then filled out later with smaller stones, and the facing stones set into them.

THE LEVER THEORY proposes that teams of skilled workers levered the stones up the courses.